BRILL
Chicken
RECIPES

KÖNEMANN

Choosing your chicken

Chicken is a versatile and affordable food that is eaten all over the world. It is a complete protein, with minerals such as potassium and phosphorus, as well as some B vitamins, and without its skin, it is relatively low in fat.

Buying chicken

Fresh and frozen
If buying fresh chicken, take it out of its packaging and store on a plate covered with plastic wrap, or in a clean plastic bag placed on a plate to catch any drips. If you're not using it straight away, place in the refrigerator, taking care not to store it on a shelf above any cooked food. The chicken should be kept cold at all times, including while you are travelling home from shopping. The chicken can also be frozen for up to 3 months by sealing it in a freezer bag with the air expelled (make sure you write the date clearly on a label). Defrost chicken carefully as bacteria, such as salmonella, can be activated if it gets too warm. Defrost in the fridge, not under running water or at room temperature. If you are defrosting in a microwave, stick to chicken pieces as whole chickens defrost unevenly. Place the chicken so that the larger part of each piece is facing outwards.

1 Preparing the chicken for the microwave.

Free-range and corn-fed
These chickens are now widely available. Free-range chickens can be identified by a label stating their place of origin and that they have been reared humanely. They have a better flavour and texture than intensively farmed chickens. Corn-fed chickens have a yellow skin and flesh, but are not necessarily free-range.

Cuts

Whole chicken
Traditionally whole chickens are roasted, but they are also delicious poached, barbecued, spit-roasted, boned and stuffed. Whole chickens are sold by a number that relates to their weight, for example, a no. 15 chicken will weigh 1.5 kg (3 lb) and should feed 4 people. Anything above that weight will feed 4–6. Poussin are the smallest type of chicken, and usually weigh 400–500 g (13 oz–1 lb) and feed 2.

To prepare a chicken for roasting, first make sure that there is nothing inside the cavity (the giblets and neck are sometimes stored in the cavity in a plastic bag). Trim off any excess fat with a pair of kitchen scissors, rinse inside the cavity, then pat dry the skin and cavity with a paper towel. Truss the chicken by tying the legs together, then tucking the wings behind the body.

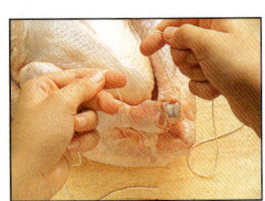

2 Trussing a whole chicken.

Choosing your chicken

The body cavity of the chicken can harbour bacteria, so if stuffing, be sure to cook the chicken straight away and check that it is cooked right through to the centre of the stuffing. Chickens can also be successfully stuffed under the skin.

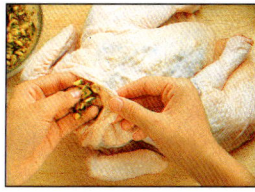

3 Stuffing the chicken under the skin.

Set the oven to moderately hot 200°C (400°F/Gas 6) and cook it for 40–45 minutes per kilo. Test by inserting a skewer into the thickest part of the thigh—if the juices run clear, the chicken is cooked. If the juices are pink, then cook for a further 10 minutes and re-test. Rest the chicken for 10 minutes before carving, wrapped in foil to allow the juices to settle.

4 Testing the chicken with a skewer.

Breast on the bone and breast fillet

These are available in singles and doubles. Breast fillet also has a tenderloin attached, which can be bought separately. Breasts are the whitest and largest portions of meat on the chicken. They can be roasted, steamed, fried, grilled and barbecued, as well as stuffed or wrapped. Be careful not to overcook as they can dry out.

Marylands

Marylands are the thigh and drumstick in one piece, and are good for baking, barbecuing, coating and frying. They take some time to cook through to the bone and need to be tested with a skewer to make sure the juices are clear. All chicken on the bone should be slashed before cooking to ensure that it cooks right through.

Thigh, thigh cutlet and thigh fillet

A thigh is a darker, more succulent meat than breast, and works well in curries and stews, and as kebabs and satays. Thigh cutlets have both skin and a thigh bone, thigh fillets have no skin or bone, and thighs have some of the backbone and 'oyster' attached.

Drumsticks

These are great as finger food and for barbecues. They are also good for children, and when cold can be used in lunchboxes or for picnics. 'Lovely legs' are drumsticks that have had their skin and knuckle removed.

5 Slashing Marylands, thighs and drumsticks.

Wings

Wings can be marinaded and then grilled, barbecued or baked to make great finger food. They are also useful for making quick chicken stocks.

Mince

Chicken mince can be used for anything that you would normally use beef or lamb mince for. Try chicken burgers, lasagne, terrines and kebabs.

Livers

Chicken livers are a rich source of iron and are delicious as a pâté or pan-fried for salads. Cut off any greenish bits during preparation and make sure you clean the livers well.

Brilliant chicken recipes

Chicken is the most versatile of foods—perfect for both an economical family dinner or a quick-and-easy meal for two.

Chicken Caesar salad

Preparation time:
   20 minutes
Total cooking time:
   20 minutes
Serves 3–4

Dressing
1/3 cup (80 ml/ 2³/4 fl oz) olive oil
1–2 cloves garlic, crushed
2 tablespoons lemon juice
6 anchovies, chopped
1 egg yolk
3 tablespoons cream

1/2 stick day-old French bread
oil, for deep-frying
3 chicken breast fillets
1 tablespoon Dijon mustard
1 cos lettuce, torn into pieces
1/4 cup (25 g/³/4 oz) Parmesan shavings

1. To make the dressing, combine all the ingredients together in a jar and shake well. Refrigerate.
2. Cut the bread into 1.5 cm (⁵/8 inch) cubes and deep-fry in batches until golden. Drain on paper towels to absorb any excess oil.
3. Preheat the grill. Trim the chicken of any excess fat or sinew. Brush lightly with the mustard and sprinkle over some ground black pepper. Grill each side for 4–6 minutes, or until the chicken is cooked in the centre. Cover and leave for a few minutes while preparing the salad.
4. Toss the lettuce, dressing and croutons together and place in a large serving dish. Slice the chicken breasts into 6–8 slices and arrange on top. Sprinkle with the Parmesan and serve while still warm.

NUTRITION PER SERVE (4)
Protein 35 g; Fat 45 g; Carbohydrate 25 g; Dietary Fibre 3 g; Cholesterol 130 mg; 2610 kJ (625 cal)

Chicken Caesar salad

❖ Brilliant Chicken Recipes ❖

Lemon baked chicken

Preparation time:
15 minutes
Total cooking time:
1 3/4 hours
Serves 4

1.5 kg (3 lb) chicken
2 lemons, roughly chopped
4 spring onions, chopped
2 tablespoons chopped fresh lemon thyme
2 cloves garlic, crushed
1 tablespoon olive oil
6 sprigs fresh lemon thyme
4 thin slices prosciutto

1. Preheat the oven to moderate 180°C (350°F/Gas 4). Trim the chicken of any excess fat, then rinse the cavity and pat dry with paper towels.
2. Place the lemons in a bowl and add the spring onions, chopped lemon thyme, garlic and some pepper and mix to combine. Spoon the mixture into the cavity of the chicken.
3. Bend the chicken wings back and tuck them behind the body. Tie the drumsticks together using string. Place in a baking dish on a rack, brush with the oil and top with the lemon thyme. Cover the breast with overlapping slices of prosciutto.
4. Cover the chicken with aluminium foil and bake for 1 1/2 hours, or until cooked through. Remove the foil and cook for a further 15 minutes, then allow the chicken to rest in a warm place for 15 minutes before carving. Discard the stuffing before serving.

NUTRITION PER SERVE
Protein 65 g; Fat 45 g; Carbohydrate 4.5 g; Dietary Fibre 2 g; Cholesterol 215 mg; 2820 kJ (675 cal)

Stir-fried sesame chicken and leek

Preparation time:
15 minutes
Total cooking time:
15 minutes
Serves 4–6

2 tablespoons sesame seeds
800 g (1 lb 10 oz) chicken tenderloins, cut into diagonal strips
1 tablespoon oil
2 teaspoons sesame oil
1 leek, white part only, julienned
2 cloves garlic, crushed
2 tablespoons soy sauce
1 tablespooon mirin or dry sherry
1 teaspoon sugar

1. Heat the wok until very hot, add the sesame seeds and dry-fry over high heat until they are golden. Remove the seeds from the wok.
2. Trim the chicken of any excess fat or sinew. Reheat the wok, add the oils and swirl them around to coat the sides. Stir-fry the chicken strips in 3 batches over high heat, tossing constantly, until just cooked. (Reheat the wok before cooking each batch of chicken.)
3. Return all the chicken to the wok, then add the leek and garlic and cook for 2–3 minutes, or until the leek is soft and golden. Check that the chicken is cooked through; if it is not, cover the pan, reduce the heat and cook for 2 minutes, or until it is cooked.
4. Add the soy sauce, mirin or sherry, sugar and the toasted sesame seeds and toss well. Season with salt and freshly ground black pepper and serve the stir-fry immediately.

NUTRITION PER SERVE (6)
Protein 35 g; Fat 35 g; Carbohydrate 8 g; Dietary Fibre 0 g; Cholesterol 160 mg; 2211 kJ (530 cal)

Lemon baked chicken (top) with Stir-fried sesame chicken and leek

❖ Brilliant Chicken Recipes ❖

Chicken laksa

Preparation time:
25 minutes
Total cooking time:
20 minutes
Serves 4

1 tablespoon oil
2–3 tablespoons ready-made laksa paste
2 x 270 ml (9 fl oz) cans coconut milk
3 cups (750 ml/24 fl oz) chicken stock
600 g (1 1/4 lb) chicken thigh fillets, cut into bite-size pieces
250 g (8 oz) dried rice vermicelli noodles
8 fried tofu puffs, cut in half on the diagonal
125 g (4 oz) bean sprouts
1 Lebanese cucumber, cut into short, thin strips
100 g (3 1/2 oz) firm tofu, sliced into 8 pieces
4 teaspoons chilli jam (chilli paste in soy bean oil)
1/4 cup (5 g/1/4 oz) fresh Vietnamese mint leaves

1. Heat the oil in a wok or heavy-based pan. Cook the paste over medium heat for 2–3 minutes or until fragrant. Add the coconut milk, stock and chicken, bring to the boil, then reduce the heat and simmer for 15 minutes, or until the chicken is cooked.
2. Bring a large pan of water to the boil. Add the noodles and cook until tender. Drain and divide among 4 deep bowls. Divide the tofu puffs and half the bean sprouts into each bowl and ladle in the soup.
3. Garnish with the remaining sprouts, cucumber, tofu, chilli jam and mint leaves. Serve with lime wedges.

NUTRITION PER SERVE
Protein 45 g; Fat 45 g; Carbohydrate 55 g; Dietary Fibre 1.5 g; Cholesterol 75 mg; 3295 kJ (785 cal)

Coconut chicken

Preparation time:
10 minutes
Total cooking time:
55 minutes
Serves 4

1/3 cup (40 g/1 1/4 oz) seasoned flour
4 chicken breasts (with bone and skin on)
2 tablespoons oil
1 onion, chopped
1 small chilli, finely chopped, optional
1 cup (250 ml/8 fl oz) coconut cream
3 tablespoons mango chutney
pinch of ground turmeric
2 tablespoons chopped fresh coriander
3 teaspoons finely shredded lime rind (see Note)
2 tablespoons lime juice

1. Preheat the oven to moderate 180°C (350°F/Gas 4). Place the seasoned flour on a sheet of greaseproof paper and toss the chicken in the flour until well coated, shaking off any excess. Heat the oil in a large heavy-based frying pan and fry the chicken, in batches, until browned on all sides. Transfer to a shallow ovenproof casserole dish.
2. Add the onion and chilli to the pan and cook over medium heat until soft. Stir in the coconut cream, mango chutney and just enough ground turmeric to make the sauce a light golden colour. Remove the pan from the heat, then slowly stir in the coriander, lime rind and lime juice.
3. Pour the sauce over the chicken. Cover and bake, basting occasionally, for about 35 minutes, or until the chicken is tender and cooked through. Serve with steamed rice.

NUTRITION PER SERVE
Protein 40 g; Fat 40 g; Carbohydrate 15 g; Dietary Fibre 2 g; Cholesterol 150 mg; 1885 kJ (450 cal)

Note: Use a zester to shred the lime rind, or grate the rind on the fine side of a cheese grater.

Chicken laksa (top) with Coconut chicken

❖ Brilliant Chicken Recipes ❖

Chicken and mushroom pillows

Preparation time:
 40 minutes +
 30 minutes cooling.
Total cooking time:
 40 minutes.
Serves 4

300 g (10 oz) chicken
 breast fillet
50 g (1³/₄ oz) butter
1 onion, finely chopped
1 clove garlic, chopped
150 g (5 oz) mushrooms,
 thinly sliced
3 teaspoons green
 peppercorns,
 drained and roughly
 chopped
3 tablespoons flour
¹/₂ cup (125 ml/4 fl oz)
 cream
¹/₂ cup (125 ml/4 fl oz)
 milk
1 tablespoon chopped
 fresh parsley
6 sheets filo pastry
olive oil, for brushing
6 tablespoons fresh
 breadcrumbs

1. Trim the chicken of any excess fat or sinew and cut into small cubes. Melt half the butter in a heavy-based pan. When foamy, add the onion, garlic and chicken and cook for 5 minutes. Add the mushrooms and peppercorns, cover and cook for 2 minutes, or until soft.
2. Add the remaining butter. When melted, add the flour and stir for 2 minutes. Remove the pan from the heat and gradually stir in the cream and milk. Return to the heat, add the parsley, salt and pepper and bring to the boil, stirring. Spread into a flat dish and allow to cool for 30 minutes.
3. Preheat the oven to moderate 180°C (350°F/Gas 4). Cover the filo with a damp tea towel. Working with one sheet at a time, lightly brush with the olive oil, top with the next sheet, brush with more oil, then top with a third sheet. Repeat with the remaining filo.
4. Cut both stacks of filo in half. Pile a quarter of the filling into the centre of each half and spread out a little. Fold the bottom of the pastry up over the filling, then bring the top down. Fold the sides in, brushing with water, and press to seal. Turn the parcels over and place on a greased baking tray. Brush the tops with a little oil and cut 2 slashes in each one. Sprinkle the breadcrumbs over the parcels with some salt.
5. Bake for 25 minutes until golden and crisp.

NUTRITION PER SERVE
Protein 25 g; Fat 30 g; Carbohydrate 40 g; Dietary Fibre 3 g; Cholesterol 115 mg; 2125 kJ (510 cal)

Chicken and mushroom pillows

1 Brush each layer of filo with some olive oil.

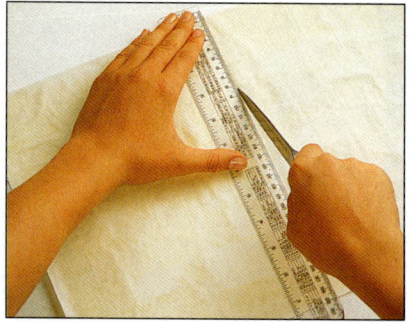

2 Cut the 2 stacks of layered filo pastry in half.

❖ **Brilliant Chicken Recipes** ❖

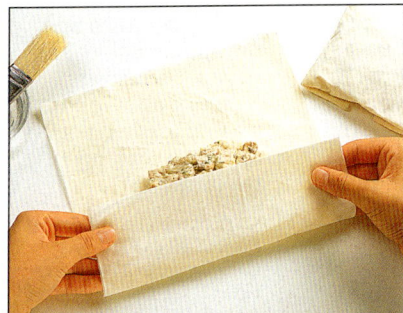

3 Fold the bottom of the pastry up over the filling, then fold down the top.

4 Place the 4 parcels on a baking tray, then brush with some oil and cut slashes.

Chicken pie

Preparation time:
  40 minutes + 30
  minutes chilling time
Total cooking time:
  50 minutes
Serves 6

90 g (3 oz) butter,
  chopped
60 g (2 oz) cream
  cheese, chopped
2 cups (250 g/8 oz)
  plain flour
2 eggs, lightly beaten
1/4 cup (60 ml/2 fl oz)
  water
2 tablespoons oil
1 leek, chopped
2 cloves garlic, crushed
2 carrots, halved and
  sliced
1 stick celery, chopped
1 cup (155 g/5 oz)
  frozen peas, thawed
1 3/4 cups (440 ml/
  14 fl oz) chicken stock
2 tablespoons plain
  flour, extra
300 g (10 oz) sour
  cream
1 large cooked chicken,
  skinned, deboned and
  cut into long strips

1. Preheat the oven to moderately hot 200°C (400°F/Gas 6). Rub the butter and cream cheese into the flour until it resembles fine breadcrumbs. Add half the egg and enough of the water to make the mixture cling together. Turn out onto a floured surface, gather the dough together and cover with plastic wrap. Chill for 30 minutes.
2. Heat the oil in a pan, add the leek and garlic and cook, stirring, for 5 minutes, or until soft. Add the carrot, celery, peas and 1 cup of the stock and simmer for 5 minutes, or until the vegetables are tender. Blend the extra flour with the remaining stock and add to the pan. Stir until the mixture boils and thickens, then remove from the heat and add the sour cream; cool. Add the chicken.
3. Cut the pastry in half and roll out one half on a lightly floured surface into a 30 cm (12 inch) round. Place on a lightly greased baking tray. Spread over the cooled filling, leaving a 2 cm (3/4 inch) border. Roll the remaining pastry into a 32 cm (13 inch) round. Brush the border of the bottom pastry with the remaining egg, cover the filling with the second pastry round and press or twist the edges together to seal. Dust with flour and cut a small slit in the top.
4. Bake for 35–40 minutes, or until golden (cover loosely with foil if browning too much).

NUTRITION PER SERVE
Protein 55 g; Fat 60 g; Carbohydrate 40 g; Dietary Fibre 5 g; Cholesterol 265 mg; 3835 kJ (915 cal)

Apricot chicken

Preparation time:
  10 minutes
Total cooking time:
  55 minutes
Serves 4

6 chicken thigh cutlets,
  skin removed
40 g (1 1/4 oz) packet
  French onion soup
  mix
425 ml (14 fl oz) can
  apricot nectar
425 g (14 oz) can
  apricot halves,
  drained

1. Preheat the oven to moderate 180°C (350°F/Gas 4). Place the chicken thighs in an ovenproof dish. Mix the soup mix with the apricot nectar and pour over the chicken.
2. Bake, covered, for 50 minutes, then add the apricot halves and bake for a further 5 minutes. Serve with creamy mashed potato or rice to soak up all the juices.

NUTRITION PER SERVE
Protein 30 g; Fat 3 g; Carbohydrate 25 g; Dietary Fibre 1.5 g; Cholesterol 60 mg; 1045 kJ (250 cal)

Chicken pie (top) with Apricot chicken

❖ Brilliant Chicken Recipes ❖

❖ Brilliant Chicken Recipes ❖

Chicken and corn chowder

Preparation time:
 15 minutes
Total cooking time:
 20 minutes
Makes 6 1/2 cups

20 g (3/4 oz) butter
5 spring onions, finely
 chopped
2 rashers bacon, finely
 chopped
1 stick celery, finely
 chopped
450 g (14 oz) potatoes,
 diced, skin removed
2 cups (500 ml/16 fl oz)
 chicken stock
1/2 cooked or BBQ
 chicken, diced
1 1/2 cups (375 ml/
 12 fl oz) milk
420 g (14 oz) can
 creamed corn
2 spring onions, finely
 sliced, to garnish

1. Melt the butter in a pan. Cook the spring onion, bacon and celery over medium heat for 2–3 minutes, without colouring. Add the potato and cook for 1–2 minutes, then add the stock. Cook for 10 minutes, or until the potato is tender.
2. Add the chicken, milk and corn. Heat without boiling and stir frequently. Season with pepper and garnish with the spring onion.

NUTRITION PER SERVE
Protein 45 g; Fat 30 g; Carbohydrate 40 g; Dietary Fibre 6 g; Cholesterol 140 mg; 590 kJ (140 cal)

Chilli barbecue chicken

Preparation time:
 30 minutes + 2–3
 hours marinating
Total cooking time:
 1 hour
Serves 4

2 x 1 kg (2 lb) chickens
2 tablespoons olive oil

Barbecue sauce
1/4 cup (60 ml/2 fl oz)
 olive oil
1/2 cup (125 ml/4 fl oz)
 tomato sauce
1 tablespoon red wine
 vinegar
2 cloves garlic, crushed
1 red onion, chopped
1 small red chilli,
 seeded and chopped
1 small green chilli,
 seeded and chopped
2 teaspoons mustard
2 teaspoons
 Worcestershire sauce
1 teaspoon dried
 oregano
pinch cayenne pepper
2 tablespoons lime juice
1–2 tablespoons sweet
 chilli sauce

1. Using a pair of scissors, cut the chickens in half lengthways along the breastbone and along each side of the backbone, discarding the backbone. Flatten gently, then thread onto metal skewers.
2. To make the barbecue sauce, place all the ingredients except the juice and chilli sauce in a pan. Cook over low heat for 10 minutes. Cool, purée in a food processor, then add the juice and chilli sauce.
3. Pour a third of the sauce into a bowl. Add the oil and brush thickly over the chickens, reserving some for basting. Cover and chill the chickens for 2–3 hours or overnight.
4. Preheat the oven to moderate 180°C (350°F/Gas 4). Place the chickens on a rack in a roasting dish filled with enough water to cover its base. Brush with the marinade and bake for 40–50 minutes, or until cooked, basting frequently. Cut into quarters and serve with the remaining sauce.

NUTRITION PER SERVE
Protein 65 g; Fat 60 g; Carbohydrate 15 g; Dietary Fibre 2 g; Cholesterol 210 mg; 3710 kJ (885 cal)

Note: The sauce is fairly mild. Increase the chilli, cayenne and chilli sauce for a more fiery flavour.

Chicken and corn chowder (top) with Chilli barbecue chicken

Open sandwiches

Chicken is a great snack food, and these open sandwiches are perfect for an easy-to-make but stylish lunch. For super-quick open sandwiches, buy a barbecue chicken and just stack up the fillings.

Chicken and chargrilled vegetable sandwich

Chargrill 2 chicken breasts, then cut into thin diagonal slices. Cut a Turkish bread loaf into 4 quarters. Brush lightly with olive oil mixed with a clove of crushed garlic. Chargrill or grill each side until lightly browned. Spread with mayonnaise and arrange purchased chargrilled vegetables such as eggplant, capsicum, zucchini and mushrooms on top. Finish with the chicken and a drizzle of pesto. *Makes 4*

NUTRITION PER SERVE
Protein 25 g; Fat 10 g; Carbohydrate 35 g; Dietary Fibre 3.5 g; Cholesterol 40 mg; 1390 kJ (330 cal)

Chicken, asparagus and prosciutto sandwich

Chargrill 2 chicken breasts, then cut into thin diagonal slices. Cut 4 slices from a sourdough loaf and brush lightly with olive oil mixed with a clove of crushed garlic. Chargrill or grill each side until lightly browned. Dry-fry 4 slices prosciutto and break into large pieces. Place 3–4 lightly cooked asparagus spears on each slice of bread and top with sliced Roma tomatoes, the chicken slices, some watercress and a dollop of mayonnaise combined with some grainy mustard. Finish with the prosciutto. *Makes 4*

NUTRITION PER SERVE
Protein 15 g; Fat 10 g; Carbohydrate 30 g; Dietary Fibre 3 g; Cholesterol 25 mg; 1165 kJ (280 cal)

Crostini with warm chicken livers and grilled capsicum

Toast 8 slices French bread and keep warm. Cut 1 small red capsicum into quarters, deseed and rub both sides with a tablespoon of oil. Grill both sides until soft, peel off the skin, then slice into thin slices. Clean 200 g (6 1/2 oz) chicken livers, then cut into pieces. Fry a crushed clove garlic in a tablespoon of butter for 30 seconds, then add the chicken livers and sauté for 4–5 minutes (the livers should be just pink in the centre). Remove. Add 2 tablespoons dry sherry and 1 teaspoon chopped fresh thyme to the pan and de-glaze for 2 minutes over gentle heat. Season. Top the bread with the livers and spoon over some juices. Arrange the strips of capsicum on top with a small sprig of thyme and freshly ground black pepper and salt. Serve warm. *Makes 8*

NUTRITION PER SERVE
Protein 15 g; Fat 10 g; Carbohydrate 12 g; Dietary Fibre 1.5 g; Cholesterol 35 mg; 875 kJ (210 cal)

Chicken and avocado salsa sandwich

Chargrill 2 chicken breasts, then cut into thin diagonal slices. Cut 4 thick slices from a crusty Italian loaf. Lightly toast or chargrill the bread. Make a salsa from 1 chopped avocado, 1 chopped peach or nectarine, 1 chopped tomato, 2 finely chopped spring onions, 1 tablespoon chopped fresh coriander and 1–2 tablespoons lemon juice. Arrange cos lettuce leaves, then chicken slices over the bread. Top each with the salsa and serve immediately. *Makes 4*

NUTRITION PER SERVE
Protein 15 g; Fat 9.5 g; Carbohydrate 30 g; Dietary Fibre 3 g; Cholesterol 20 mg; 1165 kJ (280 cal)

From left to right: Chicken and chargrilled vegetable sandwich; Chicken, asparagus and prosciutto sandwich; Crostini with warm chicken livers and grilled capsicum and Chicken and avocado salsa sandwich

Chicken bake

Preparation time:
30 minutes
Total cooking time:
1 hour 10 minutes
Serves 4

750 g (1 1/2 lb) chicken thigh fillets
30 g (1 oz) butter
1 onion, chopped
2 sticks celery, chopped
2 tablespoons flour
1 cup (250 ml/8 fl oz) chicken stock
3/4 cup (185 ml/6 fl oz) milk
120 g (4 oz) ham steak, thinly sliced
2 teaspoons wholegrain mustard
2 tablespoons chopped fresh parsley
3 hard-boiled eggs, quartered
3 potatoes, peeled and very thinly sliced
15 g (1/2 oz) butter, melted
paprika, to garnish

1. Preheat the oven to moderately hot 200°C (400°F/Gas 6). Trim the chicken of any excess fat or sinew. Melt the butter in a frying pan and cook the chicken in batches over high heat for 10 minutes, or until browned and cooked through. Remove from the pan. Add the onion and celery and cook for 5 minutes until soft, then stir in the flour.
2. Remove from the heat and gradually add the stock and milk. Return to the heat and stir until the mixture boils and thickens. Cut the chicken into bite-size pieces and add to the pan with any juices, the ham, mustard and parsley; mix well and season. Stir in the eggs.
3. Spoon the mixture into a 6-cup capacity shallow ovenproof dish. Layer the potatoes over the chicken, brush with the melted butter and sprinkle lightly with paprika.
4. Bake for 40–50 minutes until the potatoes are crisp and golden.

NUTRITION PER SERVE
Protein 55 g; Fat 20 g; Carbohydrate 20 g; Dietary Fibre 2.5 g; Cholesterol 295 mg; 295 kJ (505 cal)

Chicken and mushroom sauté

Preparation time:
15 minutes
Total cooking time:
15 minutes
Serves 4

2 tablespoons olive oil
600 g (1 1/4 lb) chicken thigh fillets, cut into bite-size chunks
2 tablespoons brandy
1/2 cup (125 ml/4 fl oz) chicken stock
300 g (10 oz) mushrooms, trimmed and thickly sliced
2 teaspoons fresh thyme leaves
3 tablespoons cream

1. Heat the oil in a heavy-based frying pan until hot. Cook the chicken, in batches, over a high heat for 4 minutes, or until browned. Reheat the pan in between batches. Remove the chicken and drain the oil from the pan.
2. Heat the pan until slightly smoking, pour in the brandy and allow to bubble until nearly evaporated. Pour in the stock and bring to the boil, then stir in the mushrooms, thyme and season well. Return the chicken to the pan with any juices. Cook for 3 minutes, or until the mushrooms are soft.
3. Stir in the cream and season to taste. Serve over fettucine or rice.

NUTRITION PER SERVE
Protein 35 g; Fat 20 g; Carbohydrate 2 g; Dietary Fibre 2 g; Cholesterol 95 mg; 1395 kJ (335 cal)

Note: Field mushrooms colour the sauce light grey. If you want a lighter colour, use button mushrooms.

Chicken bake (top) with Chicken and mushroom sauté

❖ Brilliant Chicken Recipes ❖

❖ BRILLIANT CHICKEN RECIPES ❖

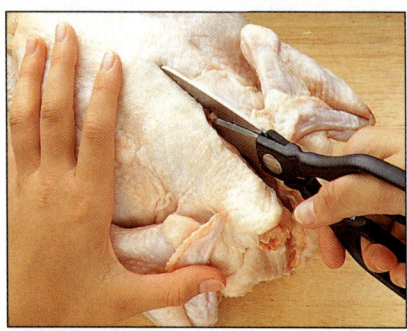

1 Cut the chicken in half along the back with a pair of kitchen scissors.

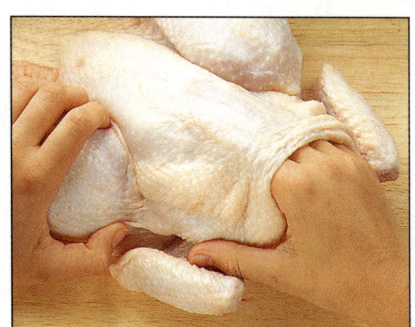

2 Loosen the skin by sliding a hand between the flesh and the skin.

Moroccan butterflied chicken

Preparation time:
  15 minutes
Total cooking time:
  1 hour
Serves 4

1.5 kg (3 lb) chicken
3 teaspoons olive oil
1 1/2 teaspoons ground cumin
1 1/2 teaspoons ground coriander

Olive and lemon stuffing
2 tablespoons finely chopped preserved lemon, rind only
1/4 cup (55 g/2 oz) chopped pitted green olives
1/4 cup (40 g/1 1/4 oz) pine nuts
2 tablespoons chopped fresh flat-leaf parsley
1 teaspoon harissa

1. Preheat the oven to moderate 180°C (350° F/Gas 4). Tuck the wings underneath the chicken, then split the chicken down the length of the back with a pair of kitchen scissors. Open the chicken out and flatten it down with your hands.
2. To make the olive and lemon stuffing, place the preserved lemon rind, green olives, pine nuts, parsley and harissa in a bowl and mix well to combine.
3. Loosen the skin covering the chicken breast and legs by sliding a hand between the flesh and the skin. Push the stuffing under the skin, working it across the breast and down to the legs. Skewer the legs to the side of the body.
4. Brush the chicken lightly with the olive oil. Combine the ground cumin and ground coriander and sprinkle over the chicken.
5. Place the chicken on a rack in a baking dish and bake for 1 hour. Test for doneness by inserting a skewer into a thigh. If the juices that run out are clear, then the chicken is cooked. If the juices are pink, bake the chicken for another 10 minutes before testing again.
6. When cooked, remove the chicken from the oven and allow to rest in a warm place for 10 minutes before carving into portions. Serve with steamed couscous or saffron rice and a leafy green salad.

NUTRITION PER SERVE
Protein 60 g; Fat 15 g; Carbohydrate 3 g; Dietary Fibre 2 g; Cholesterol 125 mg; 1160 kJ (395 cal)

Moroccan butterflied chicken

3 Push the stuffing under the skin, working it down to the legs.

4 Skewer the chicken legs to the body to help it hold its shape.

Oven-roasted chicken with garlic and potatoes

Preparation time:
35 minutes
Total cooking time:
55 minutes.
Serves 4

1.2 kg (2 lb 6¹/2 oz) chicken pieces
4 floury potatoes, unpeeled and cut into large chunks
2 tablespoons roughly chopped fresh rosemary
1 tablespoon fresh lemon thyme leaves
¹/2 cup (125 ml/4 fl oz) olive oil
3 tablespoons chicken stock
1 whole head of garlic, broken into cloves

1. Preheat the oven to moderately hot 200°C (400°F/Gas 6). Place the chicken, potatoes, herbs, oil and plenty of salt and pepper in a heavy-based baking pan.
2. Toss well and bake for 30 minutes, turning regularly and brushing the stock over the chicken to moisten. Scatter the garlic over the top and bake for a further 15–20 minutes.
3. Serve the chicken with the garlic, potatoes and the juices and oil poured over.

NUTRITION PER SERVE
Protein 45 g; Fat 35 g; Carbohydrate 15 g; Dietary Fibre 3.5 g; Cholesterol 90 mg; 2295 kJ (550 cal)

Chicken schnitzels Florentine

Preparation time:
30 minutes
Total cooking time:
45 minutes
Serves 4

Tomato Sauce
1 tablespoon olive oil
1 onion, finely chopped
2 cloves garlic, crushed
425 g (14 oz) can chopped tomatoes
¹/4 cup (60 ml/2 fl oz) white wine or water
1 teaspoon sugar
¹/2 teaspoon dried oregano
500 g (1 lb) English spinach, washed, drained and stalks removed
4 chicken breast fillets, tenderloins removed
¹/4 cup (60 ml/2 fl oz) cream
flour, for coating
30 g (1 oz) butter
1 tablespoon olive oil
90 g (3 oz) Gruyére or Cheddar, grated

1. To make the tomato sauce, heat the oil in a pan. Add the onion and garlic and cook for 5 minutes until soft. Add the tomatoes, wine, sugar and oregano and cook for 15 minutes over low heat until thick and reduced.
2. Roughly chop the spinach and place in a pan. Cook over medium heat for 2–3 minutes, or until it is wilted. Cool and squeeze dry. Fold through the cream and season.
3. Trim the chicken of any excess fat or sinew, pat dry and place each piece between 2 sheets of plastic wrap. Using a mallet or rolling pin, gently flatten out to 1.5 cm (⁵/8 inch) thick.
4. Lightly coat the chicken with the flour and shake off any excess. Heat the butter and oil in a large heavy-based frying pan. Cook the schnitzels for 2 minutes each side, or until lightly browned.
5. Top each schnitzel with the spinach and grated cheese. Pour the tomato sauce around the chicken, taking care not to cover the cheese.
6. Cover the pan and cook over low heat for 10–15 minutes, or until the cheese has melted.

NUTRITION PER SERVE
Protein 45 g; Fat 35 g; Carbohydrate 10 g; Dietary Fibre 5.5 g; Cholesterol 135 mg; 2250 kJ (540 cal)

Oven-roasted chicken with garlic and potatoes (top) with Chicken schnitzels Florentine

❖ B<small>RILLIANT</small> C<small>HICKEN</small> R<small>ECIPES</small> ❖

❖ Brilliant Chicken Recipes ❖

Chicken paella

Preparation time:
30 minutes
Total cooking time:
1 hour
Serves 4–6

2 tomatoes
4 chicken thighs, with skin on
1/4 cup (60 ml/2 fl oz) olive oil, for frying
70 g (2 1/4 oz) chorizo sausage, cut into 5 mm (1/4 inch) slices
2 cloves garlic, crushed
1 red onion, sliced
2 cups (440 g/14 oz) short-grain rice
1 red capsicum, cut into thin strips
3 cups (750 ml/24 fl oz) chicken stock
1/8 teaspoon saffron threads
1 cup (155 g/5 oz) frozen peas
12 green mussels, scrubbed and beards removed
8 raw prawns, peeled and deveined with tails intact
250 g (8 oz) squid tubes, cut into 1 cm (1/2 inch) rings

1. Score a cross on the base of the tomatoes, place in a bowl and cover with boiling water for 10 seconds. Plunge into cold water, peel, deseed and chop.
2. Cut the chicken in half along the bone, keeping the bone attached to one side. Prick the skin. Heat the oil in a large frying pan over high heat. Brown the chicken for 10 minutes, then drain on paper towels. Fry the chorizo for 2–3 minutes; drain on paper towels.
3. Add the garlic and onion and cook for 5 minutes. Add the rice and stir for 1–2 minutes until coated with oil. Add the tomatoes, chicken, chorizo and capsicum, reduce the heat and cook for 5 minutes.
4. Bring the stock, 1 cup (250 ml/8 fl oz) water and the saffron to the boil in a pan, then pour over the rice and simmer over very low heat for 10 minutes. Stir in the peas and cook, covered, for 10 minutes. Add the mussels, prawns and squid and cook, uncovered, for 10 minutes, or until all the liquid is absorbed. Do not stir at this stage as it should form a thin crust on the base.

NUTRITION PER SERVE (6)
Protein 40 g; Fat 15 g; Carbohydrate 60 g; Dietary Fibre 4 g; Cholesterol 185 mg; 2390 kJ (570 cal)

Smoked chicken and mustard linguine

Preparation time:
10 minutes
Total cooking time:
15 minutes
Serves 6

500 g (1 lb) linguine
1 smoked chicken
300 g (10 oz) sour cream
1 tablespoon wholegrain mustard
1 tablespoon chopped fresh flat-leaf parsley, to garnish

1. Bring a large pan of salted water to the boil and cook the linguine until *al dente*. Drain the pasta, reserving 1/2 cup water in case you need to thin the sauce.
2. Remove all the meat from the chicken and discard the skin and bones. Slice into pieces.
3. Place the sour cream in a frying pan and warm it over a low heat until it thins. Stir in the mustard, chicken and salt and pepper.
4. Toss the linguine into the sauce and mix well. Serve in a big bowl, sprinkled with parsley.

NUTRITION PER SERVE
Protein 50 g; Fat 45 g; Carbohydrate 60 g; Dietary Fibre 4 g; Cholesterol 205 mg; 3665 kJ (875 cal)

Chicken paella (top) with Smoked chicken and mustard linguine

Tandoori chicken

Preparation time:
10 minutes + overnight refrigeration
Total cooking time:
30 minutes
Serves 6–8

8 chicken drumsticks
8 chicken thighs
juice of 1 lemon
1 onion, finely chopped
2 cloves garlic, crushed
1 tablespoon grated fresh ginger
1–2 red chillies
1 tablespoon garam masala
1 teaspoon paprika
1/4 teaspoon salt
500 ml (16 fl oz) natural yoghurt
red and yellow food colourings
lemon wedges, to serve

1. Cut 3 slits in each piece of chicken and place in a bowl with the lemon juice; mix well.
2. Place the onion, garlic, ginger, chillies, garam masala, paprika, salt and yoghurt in a blender and blend until smooth. Add the food colouring until you have the colour you want and pour the mixture over the chicken. Cover and refrigerate overnight.
3. Preheat the oven to its highest setting. Lift the chicken out of the marinade and drain off any excess. Place on a wire rack in a baking dish and cook for 20–30 minutes (the drumsticks may take a little longer), or until they have a charred appearance around the edges. Serve with the lemon wedges.

NUTRITION PER SERVE (8)
Protein 45 g; Fat 8.5 g; Carbohydrate 4 g; Dietary Fibre 0 g; Cholesterol 120 mg; 1130 kJ (270 cal)

Spicy chicken and chickpea bake

Preparation time:
30 minutes
Total cooking time:
1 hour 10 minutes
Serves 4–6

1 teaspoon cumin seeds, lightly crushed
1 tablespoon coriander seeds, lightly crushed
1 tablespoon olive oil
1.5 kg (3 lb) chicken pieces
1 green capsicum, seeded and cut into large cubes
2 onions, sliced thickly
2 cloves garlic, chopped
1 green chilli, seeded and chopped
1/2 teaspoon saffron threads
3/4 cup (150 g/5 oz) basmati rice
1 1/2 cups (375 ml/ 12 fl oz) chicken stock
1/2 cup (125 ml/4 fl oz) white wine
grated rind and juice of a lemon
300 g (10 oz) can chickpeas, drained
50 g (1 3/4 oz) green olives

1. Preheat the oven to moderate 180°C (350° F/ Gas 4). Place a 4-litre capacity casserole dish on the stove. Dry-fry the cumin and coriander seeds for 1 minute until aromatic; set aside.
2. Heat the oil in the casserole dish. Add the chicken in 2 batches and fry for 3–4 minutes over high heat, turning, until well browned. Remove.
3. Add the capsicum, onion, garlic and chilli to the dish and stir for 3–4 minutes, without colouring. Stir in the saffron, rice and spices and cook for 1 minute.
4. Add the stock, wine, rind and juice. Slowly bring to the boil, stirring, then remove from the heat and place the chicken on top. Bake, covered, for 45 minutes until the rice is cooked. Stir in the chickpeas and olives and bake for another 5 minutes.

NUTRITION PER SERVE (6)
Protein 45 g; Fat 8.5 g; Carbohydrate 30 g; Dietary Fibre 4.5 g; Cholesterol 85 mg; 1645 kJ (395 cal)

Tandoori chicken (top) with Spicy chicken and chickpea bake

❖ Brilliant Chicken Recipes ❖

❖ Brilliant Chicken Recipes ❖

Pesto chicken

Preparation time:
20 minutes
Total cooking time:
25 minutes
Serves 4

1 cup (50 g/1³/4 oz)
  firmly packed basil
  leaves
¹/4 cup (40 g/1¹/4 oz)
  pine nuts, toasted
¹/4 cup (25 g/³/4 oz)
  grated Parmesan
¹/4 cup (60 ml/2 fl oz)
  olive oil
4 chicken breast fillets
2 teaspoons oil, extra
2 teaspoons butter
1 small onion, finely
  chopped
1 clove garlic, crushed
¹/2 cup (125 ml/4 fl oz)
  white wine
³/4 cup (185 ml/6 fl oz)
  chicken stock
1 tablespoon pine nuts,
  toasted, extra

1. Process the basil, pine nuts and Parmesan until fine. With the motor running, gradually add the oil to form a smooth paste and season.
2. Trim the chicken of any excess fat or sinew. Heat the extra oil and butter in a frying pan, add the chicken and cook over a high heat until browned. Remove from the pan and cool slightly. Cut 4 deep slashes across the chicken, three quarters of the way through. Fill each slash with a teaspoon of the pesto.
3. Cook the onion and garlic for 5 minutes until soft. Add the wine and stock, bring to the boil, then reduce the heat and simmer for 5 minutes. Return the chicken to the pan, pesto-side-up, and simmer, partly covered, for 8–10 minutes. Sprinkle with the extra pine nuts.

NUTRITION PER SERVE
Protein 40 g; Fat 35 g; Carbohydrate 2.5 g; Dietary Fibre 1.5 g; Cholesterol 85 mg; 2070 kJ (495 cal)

Chicken Parmigiana

Preparation time:
  25 minutes +
  30 minutes chilling
Total cooking time:
  35 minutes
Serves 4

4 chicken breast fillets
seasoned flour, for
  coating
dry breadcrumbs, for
  coating
1 egg, lightly beaten
1 tablespoon milk
oil, for frying
1 cup (250 g/8 oz) ready-
  made tomato pasta
  sauce
2 tablespoons shredded
  fresh basil leaves
¹/2 cup (50 g/1³/4 oz)
  grated Parmesan
100 g (3¹/2 oz)
  mozzarella cheese,
  thinly sliced

1. Trim the chicken of any excess fat or sinew and pat dry with paper towels. Place between sheets of plastic wrap and flatten with a meat mallet or rolling pin to 5 mm (¹/4 inch) thick.
2. Place the flour and breadcrumbs on 2 plates, and the egg and milk together in a shallow bowl. Coat the chicken in flour, shaking off any excess, dip in the egg and milk, drain and coat in breadcrumbs. Chill for 30 minutes.
3. Preheat the oven to moderate 180°C (350°F/Gas 4). Heat 3 cm (1¹/4 inches) of oil in a frying pan. Add the chicken and cook for 3–4 minutes each side until golden. Drain on paper towels. Place in a single layer in a greased shallow ovenproof dish.
4. Spoon the combined tomato sauce and basil over the chicken, sprinkle with Parmesan and lay the mozzarella on top. Bake for 20–25 minutes until golden.

NUTRITION PER SERVE
Protein 40 g; Fat 25 g; Carbohydrate 15 g; Dietary Fibre 1.5 g; Cholesterol 145 mg; 1950 kJ (465 cal)

Pesto chicken (top) with Chicken Parmigiana

Chicken dim sims

Preparation time:
 30 minutes
Total cooking time:
 45 minutes
Makes about 60

1 egg white
1 tablespoon cornflour
1 1/2 tablespoons soy sauce
1 teaspoon sesame oil
500 g (1 lb) chicken thigh fillets, roughly chopped
100 g (3 1/2 oz) baby bok choy, finely chopped
1/3 cup (50 g/1 3/4 oz) canned water chestnuts, chopped
1/4 cup (40 g/1 1/4 oz) finely chopped spring onions
2 tablespoons finely chopped fresh coriander
1/2 tablespoon finely grated fresh ginger
250 g (8 oz) won ton wrappers

Dipping Sauce
1/4 cup (60 ml/2 fl oz) soy sauce
1/4 cup (60 ml/2 fl oz) water
1 tablespoon fresh lime juice

1. Place the egg white in a large bowl and beat lightly. Whisk in the cornflour, soy sauce and sesame oil.
2. Place the chicken thighs in a food processor and process until finely chopped. Stir into the egg white mixture with the bok choy, water chestnuts, spring onion, coriander and ginger. Mix the ingredients thoroughly and season with salt.
3. Working with 1 wrapper at a time, place 2 teaspoons of the mixture onto the centre of each wrapper. Gather the wrapper up to the centre like a pouch, leaving the top open, and gently press down the filling to firmly pack. Tap on the bench to flatten the base.
4. Brush a steamer lightly with oil and place the dim sims in a single layer (they will need to be cooked in batches). Bring a pan of water to the boil and place the steamer on top. Cover and steam for about 15 minutes per batch.
5. To make the dipping sauce, place all the ingredients in a small bowl and stir to combine. Serve with the warm dim sims.

NUTRITION PER SERVE
Protein 1 g; Fat 0.5 g; Carbohydrate 4 g; Dietary Fibre 0.5 g; Cholesterol 4 mg; 90 kJ (20 cal)

Note: Steamers often have more than one layer, so it is possible to steam more than one batch at a time.

Chicken dim sims

1 Chop the baby bok choy and the water chestnuts.

2 Place 2 level teaspoons of the mixture on the centre of each won ton wrapper.

❖ **BRILLIANT CHICKEN RECIPES** ❖

3 Gather up the pastry to make a dim sim shape, leaving the top open.

4 Place the dim sims in a steamer and cover and steam for 15 minutes.

Mediterranean sauté

Preparation time:
  20 minutes
Total cooking time:
  25 minutes
Serves 4

4 chicken breast fillets
3 tablespoons flour
30 g (1 oz) butter
1 tablespoon olive oil
2 cloves garlic, chopped
1 tablespoon chopped fresh oregano
1 tablespoon chopped fresh sage
425 g (14 oz) can chopped tomatoes
2 tablespoons dry white wine
1/2 red capsicum, sliced
100 g (3 1/2 oz) black olives
50 g (1 3/4 oz) fetta cheese, crumbled
fresh oregano leaves, to garnish

1. Trim the chicken of any excess fat or sinew and coat lightly in flour, shaking off any excess.
2. Heat the butter, oil and garlic in a frying pan until foamy. Fry the chicken for 3 minutes each side until brown.
3. Stir in the herbs, tomato and wine, then season and scatter over the capsicum and olives. Partially cover, simmer for 10–15 minutes, then top with the fetta and oregano leaves to serve.

NUTRITION PER SERVE
Protein 40 g; Fat 20 g; Carbohydrate 10 g; Dietary Fibre 3 g; Cholesterol 105 mg; 1575 kJ (375 cal)

Chicken terrine

Preparation time:
  30 minutes + overnight refrigeration
Total cooking time:
  1 hour 40 minutes
Serves 8–10

45 g (1 1/2 oz) butter
1 large onion, finely chopped
2 cloves garlic, crushed
10 lean bacon rashers, rind removed
1 kg (2 lb) chicken mince
1/2 cup (125 ml/4 fl oz) cream
1 egg, lightly beaten
1/3 cup (50 g/1 3/4 oz) pistachio nuts, shelled
1 cup (80 g/2 3/4 oz) fresh breadcrumbs
1 tablespoon fresh rosemary leaves
1 chicken breast fillet

1. Preheat the oven to moderate 180°C (350°F/Gas 4). Grease a 14 x 21 cm (5 1/2 x 8 1/2 inch) loaf pan and line with baking paper.
2. Melt the butter in a pan, add the onion and garlic and cook over low heat for 5–10 minutes, without colouring. Cool.
3. Line the loaf pan with bacon to cover the base and sides, leaving it to hang over the edges.
4. In a bowl, combine the onion mixture with the mince, cream, egg, pistachios, breadcrumbs, rosemary and salt and pepper. Fry a small piece and taste for seasoning.
5. Trim the chicken breast of any excess fat or sinew and cut into 6 strips. Press a third of the mince mixture into the pan and lay 3 chicken strips lengthways over it. Repeat with another third of the mince and chicken, and finish with a layer of mince. Fold the bacon over the top and cover with foil.
6. Place the pan in a baking dish and add boiling water to come halfway up its sides. Bake for 1 1/2 hours, or until the juices run clear when a skewer is inserted. Remove from the dish, cover with plastic wrap and foil and place a similar size pan on top. Place cans on top to weigh down the terrine and chill overnight. Invert the pan, remove the paper, then cut into thick slices. Serve with a relish.

NUTRITION PER SERVE (10)
Protein 15 g; Fat 15 g; Carbohydrate 8 g; Dietary Fibre 1 g; Cholesterol 70 mg; 910 kJ (215 cal)

Mediterranean sauté (top) with Chicken terrine

❖ Brilliant Chicken Recipes ❖

❖ Brilliant Chicken Recipes ❖

Macadamia-crusted chicken

Preparation time:
30 minutes + 1 hour refrigeration
Total cooking time:
25 minutes
Serves 4

4 chicken breast fillets
2 tablespoons cranberry sauce
100 g (3½ oz) Camembert cheese, mashed
seasoned flour, to coat
1 egg, lightly beaten
1 tablespoon milk
1 cup (80 g/2¾ oz) fresh breadcrumbs
200 g (6½ oz) macadamia nuts, finely chopped

1. Preheat the oven to moderately hot 200°C (400°F/Gas 6). Trim the chicken of any excess fat or sinew, then cut a deep pocket in the side of each fillet. Spread 2 teaspoons of cranberry sauce inside the pocket and fill with Camembert. Secure the opening with a toothpick.
2. Place the flour on a plate, the combined egg and milk in a shallow bowl and the combined breadcrumbs and nuts on a plate. Coat the chicken in flour, shaking off any excess, then dip in the egg and milk and coat with the breadcrumbs and nuts. Refrigerate for 1 hour.
3. Place the chicken in a single layer in a greased ovenproof dish. Bake for 20–25 minutes, or until golden brown. Remove the toothpick.

NUTRITION PER SERVE
Protein 45 g; Fat 50 g; Carbohydrate 20 g; Dietary Fibre 5 g; Cholesterol 145 mg; 2995 kJ (715 cal)

Chicken fajitas

Preparation time:
35 minutes + 2 hours marinating
Total cooking time:
20 minutes
Serves 4–6

Marinade
½ cup (125 ml/ 4 fl oz) lime juice
4 cloves garlic, crushed
2 tablespoons oil
½ teaspoon salt
½ teaspoon black pepper

600 g (1¼ lb) chicken tenderloins
4 flour tortillas
2 tablespoons oil
2 red onions, thinly sliced
1 red capsicum, thinly sliced
1 green capsicum, thinly sliced

1. To make the marinade, combine the ingredients in a non-metallic bowl.
2. Trim the chicken of any excess fat or sinew and toss in the marinade. Cover and refrigerate for 2 hours.
3. Preheat the oven to moderate 180°C (350°F/Gas 4). Wrap the tortillas in foil and bake for 10 minutes to soften. Keep warm.
4. Heat half the oil in a cast-iron pan or heavy-based frying pan. Drain the chicken from the marinade and cook, in batches, over high heat for 4–5 minutes, or until charred and cooked through. Remove and keep warm. Add the remaining oil and cook the vegetables for 3 minutes.
5. Working with one tortilla at a time (and leaving the other tortillas wrapped up as you work), place a quarter of the chicken along the centre of the tortilla, top with a quarter of the vegetables and roll up to enclose the filling. Repeat with the remaining tortillas and filling. Serve with guacamole and a fresh tomato salsa.

NUTRITION PER SERVE (6)
Protein 25 g; Fat 15 g; Carbohydrate 5 g; Dietary Fibre 1 g; Cholesterol 85 mg; 840 kJ (200 cal)

Macadamia-crusted chicken (top) with Chicken fajitas

Polenta chicken with corn salsa

Preparation time:
35 minutes
+ 30 minutes soaking
Total cooking time:
40 minutes
Serves 4

1 kg (2 lb) chicken pieces
1 1/2 cups (375 ml/ 12 fl oz) milk
1/2 cup (75 g/2 1/2 oz) polenta
1/2 cup (60 g/2 oz) plain flour
1/2 teaspoon paprika
1/2 teaspoon curry powder
1/8 teaspoon cayenne pepper
oil, for frying

Salsa
1 cup (200 g/6 1/2 oz) fresh corn kernels, lightly blanched
1 tomato, diced
2 spring onions, finely sliced
1 tablespoon finely chopped fresh coriander
2 tablespoons sour cream

1. In a bowl, soak the chicken in the milk for 30 minutes. In a separate bowl, combine the polenta, flour, spices and some salt and ground black pepper.
2. Drain the chicken gently before coating with the polenta mixture.
3. In a large frying pan, heat 2 cm (3/4 inch) of oil to 180°C (350°F). Add the chicken in batches and cook on all sides for 17–20 minutes, or until cooked through and golden. Drain on paper towels.
4. To make the salsa, combine the ingredients. Serve with the chicken.

NUTRITION PER SERVE
Protein 50 g; Fat 15 g; Carbohydrate 50 g; Dietary Fibre 4 g; Cholesterol 115 mg; 2125 kJ (510 cal)

Rosemary chicken fingers on bruschetta

Preparation time:
25 minutes
Total cooking time:
15 minutes
Serves 4

Lemon mayonnaise
2/3 cup (160 g/5 1/2 oz) mayonnaise
2 tablespoons sour cream
1 tablespoon chopped fresh parsley
2 teaspoons grated fresh lemon rind

4 chicken breast fillets
1/4 cup (125 ml/4 fl oz) light olive oil
1 tablespoon chopped fresh rosemary
1 stick French bread, cut into thick diagonal slices
several butter lettuce leaves
fresh rosemary sprigs, to garnish

1. To make the lemon mayonnaise, combine all the ingredients with some black pepper. Mix well and set aside.
2. Trim the chicken of any excess fat or sinew and cut into long thin strips. Place in a bowl with half the oil, rosemary and salt and pepper; toss well.
3. Heat a cast-iron grill plate or heavy-based frying pan until smoking hot, then brush lightly with a little oil. Cook the chicken in batches, searing until golden brown and just tender. Set aside.
4. Toast the bread and brush with the remaining oil. To serve, place a lettuce leaf on each bruschetta. Place a few strips of chicken in the lettuce and drizzle over the lemon mayonnaise. Garnish with the rosemary sprigs.

NUTRITION PER SERVE
Protein 50 g; Fat 55 g; Carbohydrate 70 g; Dietary Fibre 5 g; Cholesterol 100 mg; 3950 kJ (945 cal)

Polenta chicken with corn salsa (top) and Rosemary chicken fingers on bruschetta

❖ BRILLIANT CHICKEN RECIPES ❖

❖ **BRILLIANT CHICKEN RECIPES** ❖

Chicken pizza

Preparation time:
20 minutes
Total cooking time:
20 minutes
Serves 2–4

1 red onion, sliced
1 cup (250 g/8 oz) sour cream
1 clove garlic, crushed
2 teaspoons chopped fresh thyme
1/4 cup (25 g/3/4 oz) grated Parmesan
1 cup (150 g/5 oz) cubed cooked or BBQ chicken
1 large ready-made pizza base
1 large field mushroom, thinly sliced
fi cup (75 g/2 1/2 oz) cubed mozzarella
1 teaspoon chopped fresh thyme leaves

1. Preheat the oven to moderately hot 200°C (400°F/Gas 6). Mix the onion, sour cream, garlic, thyme and Parmesan together and leave it to one side. Season the chicken with salt and pepper.
2. Place the pizza base on a baking tray and spread it with the onion mixture. Top with the mushroom, chicken and mozzarella. Bake for 15–20 minutes, or until the cheese is golden. Sprinkle with thyme.

NUTRITION PER SERVE (4)
Protein 30 g; Fat 35 g; Carbohydrate 4 g; Dietary Fibre 1 g; Cholesterol 170 mg; 1880 kJ (450 cal)

Chicken stroganoff balls

Preparation time:
15 minutes
Total cooking time:
20 minutes
Serves 4

500 g (1 lb) chicken mince
2 cloves garlic, crushed
1 small onion, grated
seasoned flour, to coat
2 tablespoons oil
30 g (1 oz) butter
1 large onion, sliced
200 g (6 1/2 oz) button mushrooms, halved
1 tablespoon sweet paprika
1 tablespoon tomato paste
2 teaspoons Dijon mustard
1/2 cup (125 ml/ 4 fl oz) white wine
1/3 cup (80 ml/ 2 3/4 fl oz) chicken stock
3/4 cup (185 g/6 oz) sour cream
2 tablespoons chopped fresh parsley

1. Combine the mince, garlic and grated onion in a bowl. Using your hands, mix well. Roll level tablespoons of the mixture into balls with lightly floured hands. Place the seasoned flour on a piece of greaseproof paper and carefully roll the balls in the flour, shaking off the excess.
2. Heat half the oil and butter in a frying pan. Cook the balls in batches over medium heat, shaking the pan frequently until brown and adding more oil when necessary. Drain on paper towels.
3. Heat the remaining oil and butter in the pan. Add the sliced onion and cook over medium heat for 3–4 minutes. Add the mushrooms and paprika and stir for 1–2 minutes. Stir in the combined tomato paste, mustard, wine and stock. Bring to the boil, reduce the heat and simmer for 5 minutes. Stir in the sour cream. Return the balls to the pan and stir until heated through. Season with salt and pepper and sprinkle with parsley. Serve with pasta.

NUTRITION PER SERVE
Protein 33 g; Fat 35 g; Carbohydrate 6 g; Dietary Fibre 3 g; Cholesterol 140 mg; 2125 kJ (510 cal)

Chicken pizza (top) with Chicken stroganoff balls

Thai green curry

Preparation time:
20 minutes
Total cooking time:
35 minutes
Serves 4

1 tablespoon oil
2 tablespoons green curry paste
400 ml (13 fl oz) can coconut cream
600 g (1 1/4 lb) chicken thigh fillets, cut into bite-size pieces
230 g (7 1/2 oz) can bamboo shoots, drained
1 tablespoon fish sauce
6 Kaffir lime leaves
2 teaspoons palm sugar or soft brown sugar
1 stalk lemon grass, white part only
2 teaspoons green peppercorns, drained
200 g (6 1/2 oz) snake beans, cut into short lengths
1/2 cup (15 g/1/2 oz) Thai basil leaves

1. Heat the oil in a wok or heavy-based pan. Add the paste and cook until fragrant. Add the coconut cream and 1 cup (250 ml/8 fl oz) water. Bring to the boil, stirring, and cook for 10 minutes over high heat until oil bubbles break the surface.
2. Add the chicken, bamboo shoots, fish sauce, lime leaves and sugar. Lightly bruise the lemon grass with the back of a knife and add. Simmer for 10 minutes, stirring occasionally. Add the peppercorns and beans and cook for 10 minutes, or until the sauce has thickened.
3. Remove the lime leaves and lemon grass and stir in the basil.

NUTRITION PER SERVE
Protein 40 g; Fat 35 g; Carbohydrate 10 g; Dietary Fibre 4 g; Cholesterol 75 mg; 2170 kJ (520 cal)

Vietnamese noodle salad

Preparation time:
40 minutes
Total cooking time:
10 minutes
Serves 4

Dressing
2/3 cup (170 ml/5 1/2 fl oz) lime juice
2 tablespoons rice or white vinegar
1/3 cup (80 ml/2 3/4 fl oz) fish sauce
2 tablespoons soft brown sugar
2 red onions, thinly sliced

200 g (6 1/2 oz) cellophane (mung bean) noodles
2 large chicken breast fillets
2 small carrots, peeled into ribbons
2 Lebanese cucumbers, peeled into ribbons
1/2 cup (15 g/1/2 oz) fresh coriander leaves
1 cup (20 g/3/4 oz) fresh mint leaves
8 iceberg lettuce leaves, shredded
1/3 cup (50 g/1 3/4 oz) roughly chopped unsalted peanuts
chilli flakes, to garnish

1. To make the dressing, place the ingredients in a bowl and whisk with a fork. Cover and set aside.
2. Place the noodles in a heatproof bowl and cover with boiling water. Soak for 5 minutes, rinse with cold water and drain. Cut into short lengths and add to the dressing.
3. Trim the chicken of any excess fat or sinew, then remove the tenderloins and steam with the breasts for 10 minutes until cooked. Shred the chicken using 2 forks and mix into the dressing with the vegetables and herbs.
4. Divide the lettuce among 4 plates. Fill with the mixture, then sprinkle over the peanuts and chilli.

NUTRITION PER SERVE
Protein 25 g; Fat 8 g; Carbohydrate 60 g; Dietary Fibre 5.5 g; Cholesterol 40 mg; 1800 kJ (430 cal)

Thai green curry (top) and Vietnamese noodle salad

❖ Brilliant Chicken Recipes ❖

❖ Brilliant Chicken Recipes ❖

Chicken, prosciutto and semi-dried tomato salad

Preparation time:
25 minutes + 20 minutes marinating
Total cooking time:
15 minutes
Serves 4

4 chicken breast fillets
1 tablespoon olive oil
2 teaspoons lemon juice
1 clove garlic, crushed
4 slices prosciutto
200 g (6 1/2 oz) mixed salad leaves
16 semi-dried tomatoes
1/3 cup (50 g/1 3/4 oz) pine nuts, toasted
1/4 cup (15 g/1/2 oz) fresh basil leaves

Dressing
3 tablespoons olive oil
1 tablespoon balsamic vinegar
1 teaspoon Dijon mustard
1 teaspoon honey

1. Trim the chicken of any excess fat or sinew and marinate in the combined oil, juice and garlic for 20 minutes. Chargrill or barbecue for 10 minutes, then thinly slice on the diagonal. Dry-fry the prosciutto until crispy and break into large pieces.
2. To make the dressing, place all the ingredients in a jar and shake well.
3. Place the salad leaves on 4 plates and arrange the chicken, tomatoes, pine nuts, basil and prosciutto on top. Drizzle with dressing.

NUTRITION PER SERVE
Protein 30 g; Fat 30 g; Carbohydrate 3 g; Dietary Fibre 1 g; Cholesterol 70 mg; 1740 kJ (415 cal)

Family chicken gratin

Preparation time:
20 minutes
Total cooking time:
35 minutes
Serve 4

50 g (1 3/4 oz) butter
1 onion, chopped
2 cloves garlic, crushed
2 rashers bacon, chopped
1/2 red capsicum, chopped
1 stick celery, chopped
1/4 cup (30 g/1 oz) plain flour
2 1/2 cups (600 ml/20 fl oz) milk
2 cups (300 g/10 oz) chopped cooked or BBQ chicken (see Note)
3 cups (555 g/1lb 2 oz) cold cooked brown or white rice
1 cup (125 g/4 oz) grated Cheddar
1/2 cup (50 g/1 3/4 oz) shredded Parmesan

1. Preheat an oven to moderate 180°C (350° F/Gas 4). Grease a 10-cup capacity ovenproof dish.
2. Heat the butter in a large pan. Cook the onion, garlic and bacon for 2–3 minutes, or until soft but not browned. Add the capsicum and celery and continue to cook for 2–3 minutes.
3. Stir in the flour and cook for 1 minute, then gradually add the milk, stirring continuously until the mixture is smooth and thick. Simmer for a further 2–3 minutes to allow the flour to cook. Stir in the chopped chicken.
4. Place the rice in a layer over the base of the prepared dish. Pour over the chicken mixture and smooth the surface with a spatula. Sprinkle with the Cheddar and Parmesan.
5. Bake for 25 minutes, or until bubbling and browned. Serve at once.

NUTRITION PER SERVE
Protein 50 g; Fat 35 g; Carbohydrate 60 g; Dietary Fibre 3 g; Cholesterol 175 mg; 3170 kJ (757 cal)

Note: Half a cooked or BBQ chicken will yield about 2 cups (300 g/10 oz) of chicken meat.

Chicken, prosciutto and semi-dried tomato salad (top) with Family chicken gratin

Chicken liver pâté

Preparation time:
10 minutes +
overnight refrigeration
Total cooking time:
15 minutes
Serves 4–6

1 onion, finely chopped
100 g (3 1/2 oz) butter, melted
1 clove garlic, crushed
1 tablespoon chopped fresh thyme
500 g (1 lb) chicken livers, cleaned
2 teaspoons green peppercorns, drained and roughly chopped
1 tablespoon brandy
6 tablespoons clarified butter or ghee
green peppercorns and fresh thyme, to decorate

1. Cook the onion in 2 tablespoons of the butter until soft. Add the garlic and thyme and cook for 1 minute, then add the livers to the pan and cook for 10 minutes, or until cooked through and firm to the touch.
2. Put the mixture in a food processor or blender and add the rest of the butter. Blend until smooth; season. Add the peppercorns and brandy and blend briefly to mix.
3. Spoon into four 1/2-cup ramekins or an earthenware dish and cover with plastic wrap, pressing the plastic wrap onto the surface of the pâté. Refrigerate overnight.
4. Cover the pâté with the clarified butter or ghee and decorate with peppercorns and thyme.

NUTRITION PER SERVE (6)
Protein 20 g; Fat 25 g; Carbohydrate 1.5 g; Dietary Fibre 1 g; Cholesterol 65 mg; 840 kJ (200 cal)

Chicken with salad greens and goats' cheese

Preparation time:
20 minutes + 20 minutes marinating
Total cooking time:
10 minutes
Serves 4

3 chicken breast fillets
1 tablespoon olive oil
2 teaspoons lemon juice
1 butter lettuce, outer leaves removed
1 curly endive, outer leaves removed
1 small cos lettuce, outer leaves removed
75 g (2 1/2 oz) rocket leaves, lower stems removed
1 cup (180 g/6 oz) seedless green grapes
125 g (4 oz) cherry tomatoes, halved
1/2 cup (60 g/2 oz) chopped pecans
150 g (5 oz) firm goats' cheese, cubed
1 tablespoon chopped fresh chives

Mustard Honey Dressing
3 tablespoons olive oil
1 tablespoon lemon juice
2 teaspoons grainy mustard
1 teaspoon honey

1. Trim the chicken of any excess fat or sinew and marinate in the combined oil and lemon juice for at least 20 minutes. Chargrill or barbecue the chicken for about 10 minutes, then cut into 2 cm (3/4 inch) cubes.
2. To make the dressing, place the ingredients in a jar and shake to combine.
3. Wash and dry the salad leaves and tear into large pieces. Place in a serving bowl, then add the chicken cubes, grapes, tomato halves, pecans and goats' cheese.
4. Pour the dressing over the salad and gently toss. Sprinkle with the chives.

NUTRITION PER SERVE
Protein 35 g; Fat 40 g; Carbohydrate 10 g; Dietary Fibre 4 g; Cholesterol 80 mg; 2295 kJ (550 cal)

Chicken liver pâté (top) and Chicken with salad greens and goats' cheese

❖ **BRILLIANT CHICKEN RECIPES** ❖

Chicken, capsicum and fetta rolls

Preparation Time:
  25 minutes
Total Cooking Time:
  25 minutes
Serves 6

6 chicken breast fillets
1 red capsicum
1 yellow capsicum
100 g (3 1/2 oz) English spinach leaves
60 g (2 oz) fetta cheese
2 tablespoons oil

1. Trim the chicken of any excess fat or sinew, then pat dry with paper towels. Place each breast fillet between 2 sheets of plastic wrap and flatten with a meat mallet or rolling pin to about a 5 mm (1/4 inch) thickness.
2. Cut the capsicums into large pieces and remove the seeds and membrane. Place on a baking tray under a preheated grill until the skin has blackened and blistered. Place in a plastic bag to cool. When the capsicum pieces have cooled, peel away the skin. Cut into 4 cm (1 1/2 inch) wide strips.
3. Trim and wash the spinach leaves and place in a pan, with just the water clinging to the leaves. Cover and cook over low heat until just wilted. Drain the spinach in a colander and squeeze out any excess liquid by placing the spinach between 2 equal-sized plates and pressing them together.
4. Place the chicken skinned-side-down on a work surface and lay the strips of red and yellow capsicum evenly on top of it, close to one end of each fillet. Spread the wilted spinach over the capsicum, then crumble the fetta cheese over the top.
5. Starting at the same end, roll each breast fillet up, enclosing the filling. Tie the chicken with string at intervals along the roll to keep it together during cooking. Poke the chicken in at the ends and tie around the chicken lengthways to keep secure.
6. Heat the oil in a frying pan, add the chicken rolls and cook over medium heat, turning frequently, until browned all over and cooked through. Remove the string and cut into 2 cm (3/4 inch) slices. Serve with a mixed green salad.

NUTRITION PER SERVE
Protein 35 g; Fat 10 g; Carbohydrate 1.5 g; Dietary Fibre 1 g; Cholesterol 80 mg; 1100 kJ (265 cal)

Chicken, capsicum and fetta rolls

1 Place the chicken in plastic wrap and flatten with a meat mallet or rolling pin.

2 Place the capsicum, spinach and fetta at one end of the chicken breasts.

❖ **BRILLIANT CHICKEN RECIPES** ❖

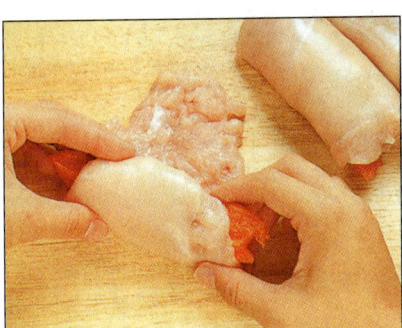

3 Roll up the chicken breasts, starting from the end with the filling.

4 Tie the chicken at intervals along the roll, then tie lengthways to secure.

47

Baked chicken vermicelli

Preparation time:
20 minutes
Total cooking time:
45 minutes
Serves 6

125 g (4 oz) butter
2 onions, finely chopped
350 g (11 oz) mushrooms, sliced
2 red capsicums, chopped
3 tablespoons flour
1 cup (250 ml/8 fl oz) milk
1/2 cup (125 ml/4 fl oz) cream
1/2 cup (125 ml/4 fl oz) chicken stock
1 large cooked or BBQ chicken
3 chorizo sausages, sliced
300 g (10 oz) vermicelli
1 cup (100 g/3 1/2 oz) grated Parmesan

1. Melt half the butter and gently fry the onion, mushrooms and red capsicum until softened.
2. In a separate pan, melt the remaining butter, stir in the flour and season. Remove from the heat and gradually stir in the milk, cream and stock. Stir until the sauce boils and is thick enough to coat the back of a spoon.
3. Preheat the oven to moderate 180°C (350°F/Gas 4). Remove the skin and bones from the chicken; chop the meat. Add to the sauce with the chorizo and vegetables.
4. Cook the pasta until *al dente*. Drain, then mix with the chicken and half the cheese. Spoon into a casserole dish and sprinkle with the rest of the cheese. Cover and bake for 25 minutes.

NUTRITION PER SERVE
Protein 60 g; Fat 60 g; Carbohydrate 50 g; Dietary Fibre 5.5 g; Cholesterol 265 mg; 4625 kJ (1105 cal)

Chicken Kiev

Preparation time:
35 minutes
+ 2 hours chilling
Total cooking time:
20 minutes
Serves 6

125 g (4 oz) butter, softened
1 clove garlic, crushed
2 tablespoons chopped fresh parsley
2 teaspoons lemon juice
2 teaspoons grated lemon rind
6 chicken breast fillets, tenderloins removed
1/2 cup (60 g/2 oz) plain flour
4 cups (400 g/13 oz) dry breadcrumbs
2 eggs, beaten
1/4 cup (60 ml/2 fl oz) milk
lemon wedges, to serve

1. Combine the butter, garlic, parsley, lemon juice and rind. Transfer the mixture to a sheet of foil and shape into a rectangle about 5 x 8 cm (2 x 3 inches). Fold the foil to enclose and chill until firm.
2. Trim the chicken of any excess fat or sinew and place between 2 sheets of plastic wrap. Use a meat mallet or rolling pin to flatten the chicken to a 5 mm (1/4 inch) thickness.
3. Cut the chilled butter into 6 pieces. Place a piece in the centre of each breast, fold in the edges and roll up to enclose. Fasten with toothpicks and chill until firm. Place the flour and breadcrumbs on separate plates or baking paper.
4. Toss the chicken in the flour, dip in the combined egg and milk and coat with the breadcrumbs. Chill for 1 hour, then toss in the egg and breadcrumbs again. Half fill a heavy-based frying pan with oil and fry in batches for 5 minutes on each side until golden and cooked through. Drain on paper towels, remove the toothpicks and serve with the lemon.

NUTRITION PER SERVE
Protein 40 g; Fat 30 g; Carbohydrate 50 g; Dietary Fibre 3 g; Cholesterol 175 mg; 2620 kJ (625 cal)

Baked chicken vermicelli (top) with Chicken Kiev

❖ BRILLIANT CHICKEN RECIPES ❖

❖ **BRILLIANT CHICKEN RECIPES** ❖

Chicken and herb koftas

Preparation time:
20 minutes
Total cooking time:
10 minutes
Serves 4–6

500 g (1 lb) chicken mince
1 onion, grated
1/4 cup (15 g/1/2 oz) chopped fresh parsley
1 tablespoon chopped garlic chives
1 tablespoon chopped fresh thyme
1 egg, lightly beaten
1/2 cup (40 g/1 1/4 oz) fresh breadcrumbs
20 g (3/4 oz) butter
1 tablespoon oil
hummus, to serve
8 pitta breads, to serve
tabbouleh, to serve
chilli sauce, optional

1. Combine the chicken mince, onion, herbs, egg, breadcrumbs and some salt and pepper in a large bowl and mix well using your hands. Divide the mixture into 8 equal portions.
2. Roll each portion into a sausage shape with lightly floured hands. Melt the butter and oil in a frying pan and cook the koftas over medium heat, turning frequently, until golden brown and cooked through.
3. To serve, spread the hummus over the pitta bread, spoon over the tabbouleh and top with a kofta. Add chilli sauce if desired, roll up and serve.

NUTRITION PER SERVE (4)
Protein 35 g; Fat 15 g; Carbohydrate 25 g; Dietary Fibre 3 g; Cholesterol 120 mg; 1575 kJ (375 cal)

Chicken pawpaw salad with curry dressing

Preparation time:
25 minutes + 20 minutes marinating
Total cooking time:
10 minutes
Serves 4

4 small chicken breast fillets
1 tablespoon olive oil
2 teaspoons soy sauce
1 clove garlic, crushed
750 g (1 1/2 lb) pawpaw, seeded and peeled and chopped into 2 cm (3/4 inch) cubes
1 red capsicum, seeded and thinly sliced
1 yellow capsicum, seeded and thinly sliced
1 small fennel bulb, thinly sliced
1/3 cup (50 g/1 3/4 oz) macadamia nuts, lightly toasted and chopped
1/3 cup (20 g/3/4 oz) chopped mint
lemon wedges, to serve

Curry Dressing
3/4 cup (185 g/6 oz) whole-egg mayonnaise
1 cup (250 g/8 oz) plain yoghurt
1 teaspoon soy sauce
1/2–1 teaspoon curry powder, to taste

1. Trim the chicken of any excess fat or sinew, then coat with the combined oil, soy and garlic. Marinate for at least 20 minutes. Chargrill or barbecue each side for 3–4 minutes, then thinly slice on the diagonal.
2. To make the curry dressing, combine all the ingredients in a bowl, adding curry powder to taste.
3. Combine the pawpaw and vegetables in a bowl and fold through half the dressing. Arrange the salad on a plate, top with the chicken and a dollop of the remaining dressing. Sprinkle with the macadamias and mint and serve with lemon wedges.

NUTRITION PER SERVE
Protein 35 g; Fat 20 g; Carbohydrate 15 g; Dietary Fibre 6 g; Cholesterol 75 mg; 1550 kJ (370 cal)

Chicken and herb koftas (top) and Chicken pawpaw salad with curry dressing

Golden jewelled couscous

Preparation time:
  30 minutes
Total cooking time:
  20 minutes
Serves 4

50 g (1³/4 oz) butter
1 tablespoon oil
2 large onions, thinly sliced
2 teaspoons ground cumin
1 teaspoon ground coriander
1 teaspoon paprika
¹/2 teaspoon turmeric
¹/2 teaspoon cinnamon
300 g (10 oz) chicken thigh fillets, cut into thin strips
2 cups (500 ml/16 fl oz) chicken stock
2 cups (370 g /12 oz) couscous
50 g (1³/4 oz) sun-dried capsicum, chopped
3 tablespoons currants
1 carrot, grated
2 tablespoons pine nuts, toasted
lemon wedges, to serve

1. Melt the butter and oil in a large heavy-based pan over medium heat until foamy. Add the onion and spices and cook for 4 minutes, stirring occasionally. Remove from the pan with a slotted spoon.
2. Add the chicken and cook to lightly brown. Return the onion to the pan with the stock.
3. Cover and bring to the boil. Sprinkle in the couscous and stir well. Cover again, remove from the heat and stand for 3 minutes until the liquid is absorbed.
4. Fluff up the couscous with a fork, stir in the capsicum (and any oil), currants, carrot and season. Scatter over the pine nuts and serve with the lemon.

NUTRITION PER SERVE
Protein 25 g; Fat 25 g; Carbohydrate 55 g; Dietary Fibre 4 g; Cholesterol 70 mg; 2245 kJ (535 cal)

Tarragon chicken

Preparation time:
  25 minutes
Total cooking time:
  1 hour
Serves 4

8 chicken pieces, about 1.2 kg (2 lb 6¹/2 oz)
20 g (³/4 oz) butter
1 tablespoon oil
8 cloves garlic, peeled
1 onion, cut in wedges
2 rashers bacon, chopped
1 cup (250 ml/8 fl oz) chicken stock
¹/4 cup (60 ml/2 fl oz) tarragon vinegar
¹/4 teaspoon dried tarragon
1 tablespoon cornflour
¹/2 cup (125 ml/ 4 fl oz) cream
¹/4 cup (5 g/¹/4 oz) fresh tarragon leaves

1. Remove any excess fat from the chicken and pat dry with paper towels. Heat the butter and oil in a 4-litre heavy-based pan or casserole dish. Cook the chicken in batches for 5–8 minutes until browned. Set aside.
2. Add the garlic, onion and bacon to the pan. Cook for 3 minutes until soft but not brown. Add the stock, vinegar and tarragon and bring slowly to the boil.
3. Add the chicken. Cover and simmer for 40 minutes, or until the chicken is cooked, then remove the chicken from the pan. Add the combined cornflour, cream and half the tarragon to the sauce, bring to the boil and stir until smooth and thick. Season with pepper. Return the chicken to the sauce, cover and simmer for 10 minutes. Sprinkle with the remaining tarragon.

NUTRITION PER SERVE
Protein 40 g; Fat 25 g; Carbohydrate 5.5 g; Dietary Fibre 1.5 g; Cholesterol 145 mg; 1820 kJ (435 cal)

Golden jewelled couscous (top) with Tarragon chicken

❖ **BRILLIANT CHICKEN RECIPES** ❖

❖ BRILLIANT CHICKEN RECIPES ❖

1 Remove the legs from the chicken by cutting around the thigh joint.

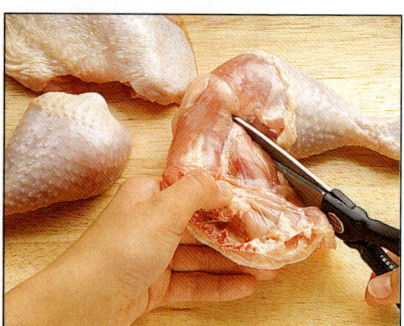

2 Separate the drumstick from the thigh by cutting along the fat line.

Coq au vin

Preparation time:
  40 minutes
Total cooking time:
  1 hour 20 minutes
Serves 4

1.6 kg (3 1/4 lb) chicken
30 g (1 oz) butter
1 tablespoon oil
12 pickling onions
12 button mushrooms
3 bacon rashers, rind
  removed and chopped
1 carrot, sliced
1 onion, sliced
2 tablespoons brandy
2 cups (500 ml/16 fl oz)
  good-quality red wine
3/4 cup (185 ml/6 fl oz)
  chicken stock
1 bouquet garni
2 tablespoons flour
2 tablespoons butter,
  extra

1. Remove the legs from the chicken by cutting around the thigh joint, twisting to break the joint, then cutting through. Separate the thighs from the drumsticks by cutting through the joint along the fat line. Cut up either side of the backbone and discard. Cut lengthways through the breast bone, then cut each breast in half. Cut off the wing tips through the joint.
2. Heat half the butter and oil in a frying pan and cook the onions for 5–8 minutes until brown; remove. Fry the mushrooms and bacon until browned. Set aside.
3. Heat the remaining butter and oil in a heavy-based pan, add the carrot and onion and cook over high heat until browned. Set aside. Add the chicken and fry for 5 minutes until golden. Remove the pan from the heat, swirl in the brandy, then add the wine, stock, bouquet garni and carrot and onion mixture. Bring to the boil, reduce the heat and simmer, covered, for 35–40 minutes, or until the chicken is tender. Remove, strain the sauce and discard the vegetables.
4. Combine the flour and butter to form a paste. Return the sauce to the pan and slowly whisk in the paste. Add the chicken, onions, mushrooms and bacon and simmer for 5–10 minutes to heat up.

NUTRITION PER SERVE
Protein 65 g; Fat 25 g; Carbohydrate 15 g; Dietary Fibre 2.5 g; Cholesterol 185 mg; 2770 kJ (660 cal)

Note: Make a bouquet garni by placing 2 bay leaves, 2 thyme sprigs, 2 parsley stalks and 6 peppercorns in half a stalk of celery. Cover with the other half and tie firmly with string.

Coq au vin

3 Cut the chicken lengthways through the breast bone.

4 Your chicken should now be in 8 pieces. Discard the wing tips.

Chicken and sweet potato frittata

Preparation time:
25 minutes
Total cooking time:
50 minutes
Serves 4

1 small red capsicum, seeded and halved
30 g (1 oz) butter
1 red onion, chopped
2 cloves garlic, crushed
350 g (11 oz) orange sweet potato, diced
2 cups (130 g/4 1/2 oz) chopped English spinach
2 cups (300 g/10 oz) chopped cooked or BBQ chicken
100 g (3 1/2 oz) feta, crumbled
1/2 cup (30 g/1 oz) chopped fresh basil
6 eggs, lightly beaten

1. Place the capsicum under a preheated grill. Grill for 8 minutes until blackened, cool, peel, then slice the flesh.
2. Heat the butter in a heavy-based ovenproof frying pan, 22 cm (9 inches) across the base and 25 cm (10 inches) across the top. Cook the onion and garlic for 2–3 minutes until soft. Add the sweet potato and cook over low heat for 10 minutes, stirring frequently until cooked.
3. Stir in the spinach, chicken, feta, capsicum and basil. Smooth the surface, then pour on the eggs. Cook over low heat for 15 minutes or until almost set.
4. Put the frittata under the grill. Cook the top for 10–15 minutes until set. Cut into wedges.

NUTRITION PER SERVE
Protein 40 g; Fat 25 g; Carbohydrate 15 g; Dietary Fibre 3 g; Cholesterol 375 mg; 1765 kJ (420 cal)

Chicken noodle soup

Preparation time:
30 minutes
Total cooking time:
2 hours 15 minutes
Serves 4

Stock
1.6 kg (3 1/4 lb) chicken
1 onion, quartered
2 leeks, green part only, chopped
2 carrots, chopped
2 bay leaves
small bunch parsley
6 peppercorns
pinch of salt

1/2 carrot, diced
1/2 onion, diced
1/2 leek, white part only, chopped
1 cup (75 g/2 1/2 oz) crushed egg noodles
15 green beans, chopped
1/2 cup (70 g/2 1/2 oz) peas
1/4 cup (7 g/1/4 oz) chopped fresh parsley

1. To make the stock, place the ingredients in a large pan with 2.5 litres cold water. Bring to the boil and skim off any scum from the surface with a slotted spoon. Reduce the heat and simmer for 2 hours. Remove the chicken and set aside to cool. Strain the stock and measure. If it is more than 1.5 litres, return to the cleaned pan to reduce it. If you are not using the stock immediately, cool and refrigerate overnight (skimming the fat will then be easier as it will solidify). Remove the meat from the chicken bones and dice it.
2. To make the soup, bring the stock to the boil in a large pan and season. Add the carrot, onion and leek and simmer for 3 minutes. Add the noodles and cook for 4–5 minutes. Add the beans, peas and chicken and cook for 3 minutes. Stir in the parsley to serve.

NUTRITION PER SERVE
Protein 70 g; Fat 40 g; Carbohydrate 20 g; Dietary Fibre 5.5 g; Cholesterol 210 mg; 2915 kJ (695 cal)

Chicken and sweet potato frittata (top) with Chicken noodle soup

❖ **BRILLIANT CHICKEN RECIPES** ❖

❖ BRILLIANT CHICKEN RECIPES ❖

Normandy chicken

Preparation time:
  30 minutes
Total cooking time:
  40 minutes
Serves 4

20 chicken tenderloins
  or 4 breast fillets
1 tablespoon olive oil
1 clove garlic, crushed
4 green apples
50 g (1¾ oz) butter
2 tablespoons lemon
  juice
1 tablespoon brown
  sugar
¼ cup (60 ml/2 fl oz)
  Calvados or brandy
⅓ cup (80 ml/
  2¾ fl oz) cream
4 slices prosciutto
¼ cup (15 g/½ oz)
  chopped fresh parsley

1. Trim the chicken of any excess fat or sinew, place in a dish and coat with the oil and garlic.
2. Peel, core and cut each apple into 8 wedges. Melt the butter in a pan and add the apple, juice and sugar. Cook over medium heat for 25–30 minutes, turning occasionally, until caramelized.
3. Add the alcohol. Heat for 30 seconds, then, if using gas, move the pan to the side of the flame and tilt until the liquor catches. If using electricity, light with a long match. Take care and never pour liquor directly from the bottle. When the flames subside, stir in the cream.
4. Dry-fry the prosciutto until crisp, then break into large pieces. Heat a heavy-based pan and cook the chicken on both sides until browned and cooked through. Serve with the apple, prosciutto and parsley sprinkled over.

NUTRITION PER SERVE
Protein 35 g; Fat 30 g; Carbohydrate 25 g; Dietary Fibre 3.5 g; Cholesterol 135 mg; 2165 kJ (520 cal)

Chicken risotto

Preparation time:
  20 minutes
Total cooking time:
  40 minutes
Serves 4

1.25–1.5 litres chicken
  stock
¼ cup (60 ml/2 fl oz)
  olive oil
50 g (1¾ oz) butter
2 onions, finely
  chopped
2 cups (440 g/14 oz)
  arborio rice
4 tablespoons chopped
  fresh parsley
2 tablespoons chopped
  fresh chives
2 tablespoons chopped
  fresh basil
1 tablespoon chopped
  fresh sage
175 g (6 oz) grated
  Parmesan
3 chicken breast fillets
fresh chives, to garnish

1. Bring the stock to the boil in a pan, partially cover and reduce to a simmer.
2. Heat half the oil and butter in a heavy-based pan. Cook the onion for 4 minutes until tender. Add the rice and stir for 2 minutes to coat with the oil and butter.
3. Add a ladle of stock and stir until the liquid is absorbed. Continue adding the stock a ladle at a time, stirring until it has all been absorbed and the rice is creamy and tender (this will take about 20 minutes). Stir in the herbs, half the cheese and cover.
4. Trim the chicken of any excess fat or sinew and cut into pieces. Add the remaining oil and butter to a frying pan. Add the chicken in 2 batches, and cook for 5 minutes, or until golden. Season.
5. Combine the chicken with the risotto and top with the chives and the Parmesan.

NUTRITION PER SERVE
Protein 50 g; Fat 55 g; Carbohydrate 80 g; Dietary Fibre 4 g; Cholesterol 130 mg; 4370 kJ (1045 cal)

Normandy chicken (top) with Chicken risotto

Chicken burgers

Preparation time:
40 minutes +
2 hours marinating
Total cooking time:
20 minutes
Serves 4

1/3 cup (80 ml/2 3/4 fl oz) extra virgin olive oil
2 cloves garlic, crushed
3 teaspoons chopped oregano
3 teaspoons chopped marjoram
1 zucchini, thinly sliced lengthwise
200 g (6 1/2 oz) sweet potato, thinly sliced lengthwise
1 red capsicum, sliced into long thick slices
500 g (1 lb) chicken mince
2 tablespoons mango chutney
1 onion, finely chopped
1/2 cup (40 g/1 1/4 oz) fresh breadcrumbs
Turkish bread, to serve

1. Combine the oil, half the garlic, the oregano, marjoram, zucchini, sweet potato and capsicum in a shallow dish. Toss to combine well. Cover and marinate for 2 hours.
2. Place the mince, mango chutney, onion, breadcrumbs, remaining garlic and salt and pepper into a large bowl. Use your hands to combine the mixture well. Divide the mixture into 4 portions and shape into patties with lightly oiled hands. Place on a plate, cover with plastic wrap and refrigerate.
3. Cook the vegetables in a heavy-based or chargrill pan until tender, brushing with the oil while cooking. Set aside.
4. Cook the burgers in the pan for 5 minutes on each side, or until browned and cooked through. To serve, toast the Turkish bread and fill with the burger and vegetables.

NUTRITION PER SERVE
Protein 30 g; Fat 25 g; Carbohydrate 20 g; Dietary Fibre 3 g; Cholesterol 60 mg; 1730 kJ (415 cal)

Chicken lasagne

Preparation time:
30 minutes
Total cooking time:
50 minutes
Serves 4

1 clove garlic, crushed
1 tablespoon oil
250 g (8 oz) frozen spinach, thawed
50 g (1 3/4 oz) butter
50 g (1 3/4 oz) flour
2 cups (500 ml/16 fl oz) milk
1 cup (125 g/4 oz) grated Cheddar
2 cups (300 g/10 oz) diced cooked or BBQ chicken
3 sheets fresh lasagne
fi cup (60 g/2 oz) grated Cheddar, extra

1. Preheat the oven to moderate 180°C (350°F/Gas 4). Fry the garlic in the oil, then add the spinach and cook until the water has evaporated. Season and set aside.
2. Melt the butter, stir in the flour and cook for 1 minute. Add the milk gradually, stirring, then bring to the boil and cook for 2 minutes. Stir in the cheese, season and cool.
3. Add 1/2 cup of the cheese sauce to the spinach and put 1/3 of the spinach mixture into an ovenproof dish. Cover with a sheet of lasagne, then another 1/3 of the spinach mixture. Sprinkle over half the chicken and cover with lasagne. Repeat with the remaining spinach, chicken and lasagne, and finish by pouring on the cheese sauce.
4. Sprinkle over the extra cheese and bake for 30–40 minutes.

NUTRITION PER SERVE
Protein 40 g; Fat 40 g; Carbohydrate 15 g; Dietary Fibre 3.5 g; Cholesterol 165 mg; 2435 kJ (582 cal)

Chicken burgers (top) with Chicken lasagne

❖ Brilliant Chicken Recipes ❖

❖ BRILLIANT CHICKEN RECIPES ❖

Finger food

These ideas for party and snack food all involve marinating chicken to add extra flavour and to keep the meat moist and tender. Marinade the chicken up to a day in advance, then just grill or bake it before serving.

Yakitori

Soak 12 bamboo skewers in water. Cut 6 chicken thigh fillets into small cubes. Wipe clean 24 button mushrooms and cut 6 spring onions into short lengths. Thread pieces of chicken, mushrooms and spring onions onto the skewers. Mix together 1/2 cup (60 ml/2 fl oz) light soy sauce, 1/3 cup (80 ml/2 3/4 fl oz) dry sherry, 2 tablespoons soft brown sugar and 1–2 crushed cloves garlic. Pour over the skewers. Marinate for at least 1 hour. Place the skewers on a preheated grill and cook for 8–10 minutes, turning and basting. Serve with soy sauce. *Makes about 12*

NUTRITION PER SERVE
Protein 11 g; Fat 2 g; Carbohydrate 2 g; Dietary Fibre 0.5 g; Cholesterol 20 mg; 305 kJ (75 cal)

Teriyaki

Soak 12 bamboo skewers in water. Cut 500 g (1 lb) chicken tenderloins in half lengthways. In a bowl, combine 2 tablespoons oil, 1/4 cup (60 ml/2 fl oz) light soy sauce, 1/3 cup (80 ml/2 3/4 fl oz) dry sherry, 2 tablespoons soft brown sugar, 1–2 cloves garlic and 2 teaspoons grated fresh ginger. Add the chicken, mix well, cover and refrigerate for 2 hours. Cut 1 red capsicum into cubes and 4 spring onions into short lengths. Thread the chicken, capsicum and spring onion alternately onto the skewers. Brush with oil and cook on a preheated grill for 6–8 minutes, turning and basting with oil frequently. *Makes about 12*

NUTRITION PER SERVE
Protein 7.5 g; Fat 3 g; Carbohydrate 2 g; Dietary Fibre 0 g; Cholesterol 15 mg; 300 kJ (70 cal)

Satay

Soak 16 bamboo skewers in water. Cut 500 g (1 lb) chicken tenderloins in half lengthways. In a bowl, combine 1 tablespoon honey, 1/4 cup (60 ml/2 fl oz) soy sauce, 2 teaspoons sesame oil, 1 teaspoon each ground coriander and turmeric and 1/2 teaspoon chilli powder. Thread the chicken lengthways onto skewers and place in the marinade. Cover and refrigerate for at least 2 hours. To make the peanut sauce, fry a small finely chopped onion in 1 tablespoon oil until soft, then stir in 1/2 cup (125 g/4 oz) crunchy peanut butter, 1 tablespoon soy sauce, 1/2 cup (125 ml/4 fl oz) coconut cream and 2 tablespoons sweet chilli sauce. Cook gently until heated through. To cook the satays, place the skewers on a preheated grill and cook for 5–7 minutes, turning and basting with marinade frequently. Serve with the warm peanut sauce. *Makes about 16*

NUTRITION PER SERVE
Protein 10 g; Fat 9 g; Carbohydrate 3.5 g; Dietary Fibre 1.5 g; Cholesterol 15 mg; 570 kJ (135 cal)

Devilled chicken wings

Combine 1 teaspoon Dijon mustard, 1 clove crushed garlic, 2 tablespoons hoisin sauce, 1 tablespoon Worcestershire sauce, 2 tablespoons tomato sauce, 1 tablespoon lemon juice and a few drops of Tabasco in a large bowl. Season 12 chicken wings and add them to the bowl, toss together and cover with plastic wrap. Refrigerate for 2 hours or overnight. Preheat the oven to moderately hot 200°C (400°F/Gas 6). Arrange the wings on a wire rack above a baking tray and bake for 30–40 minutes or until the wings are browned and cooked. *Serves 4*

NUTRITION PER SERVE
Protein 8 g; Fat 4.5 g; Carbohydrate 8 g; Dietary Fibre 1.5 g; Cholesterol 25 mg; 430 kJ (105 cal)

From left to right: Yakitori; Teriyaki; Satay; Devilled chicken wings

Index

Apricot chicken 12

Baked chicken vermicelli, 48
Burgers, chicken, 60
Buying chicken, 2

Caesar salad dressing, 4
Chicken and avocado salsa sandwich, 17
Chicken and chargrilled vegetable sandwich, 16
Chicken and herb koftas, 51
Chicken and mushroom pillows, 10
Chicken and mushroom sauté, 18
Chicken and sweet potato frittata, 56
Chicken bake, 18
Chicken burgers, 60
Chicken Caesar salad, 4
Chicken dim sims, 30
Chicken fajitas, 35
Chicken Kiev, 48
Chicken laksa, 8
Chicken lasagne, 60
Chicken liver paté, 44
Chicken noodle soup, 56
Chicken paella, 25
Chicken Parmigiana, 29
Chicken pawpaw salad with curry dressing, 51
Chicken pie, 12
Chicken pizza, 39
Chicken risotto, 59
Chicken schnitzels Florentine, 22
Chicken stroganoff balls, 39
Chicken terrine, 32
Chicken with salad greens and goats' cheese, 44
Chicken, asparagus and prosciutto sandwich, 16
Chicken, capsicum and fetta rolls, 46–7
Chicken, prosciutto and semi-dried tomato salad, 43
Chilli barbecue chicken, 15
Choosing your chicken, 2–3
Coconut chicken, 8
Coq au vin, 54–5
Corn salsa, 36
Crostini with warm chicken livers and grilled capsicum, 17
Curry dressing, 51
Curry, Thai green, 40
Cuts of chicken, 2–3

Dipping sauce for dim sims, 30
Dressings and sauces
Caesar salad, 4
curry, 51
for dim sims, 30
mustard honey, 44

Family chicken gratin, 3

Golden jewelled couscous, 52

Koftas, chicken and herb, 51

Lasagne, chicken, 60
Lemon baked chicken, 6

Macadamia-crusted chicken, 35
Mediterranean sauté, 32
Moroccan butterflied chicken, 21
Mustard honey dressing, 44

Normandy chicken, 59

Open sandwiches, 16–17
Oven-roasted chicken with garlic and potatoes, 22

Pasta
Baked chicken vermicelli, 48
Chicken lasagne, 60
Smoked chicken and mustard linguini, 25
Vietnamese noodle salad, 40
Paté, chicken liver, 44
Pesto chicken, 29
Pie, chicken, 12
Pizza, chicken, 39
Polenta chicken with corn salsa, 36

Rosemary chicken fingers on bruschetta, 36

Salad
Chicken Caesar, 4
Chicken pawpaw, with curry dressing, 51
Chicken, prosciutto and semi-dried tomato, 43
Vietnamese noodle, 40
Salsa, corn, 36
Smoked chicken and mustard linguini, 25
Soup, chicken noodle, 56
Spicy chicken and chickpea bake, 26
Stir-fried sesame chicken and leek, 6

Tandoori chicken, 26
Tarragon chicken, 52
Thai green curry, 40

Vietnamese noodle salad, 40